How Shea Sees It:
A Poetry Book

Shea S. Davis

BookLeaf Publishing

India | USA | UK

Presentation by *BookLeaf Publishing*

Web: www.bookleafpub.com

E-mail: info@bookleafpub.com

ISBN: 9789358319644

First edition 2023

To, Sharon Davis

Thank you for creating a path forward. I hope I can honor you and spread your legacy wherever I go.

ACKNOWLEDGEMENT

To, Cassey
Thank you for being my best friend from day one.

To, Leslie
I'm grateful our souls reconnected.

PREFACE

This book is filled with a raw collection of emotions. Some of the topics discussed might be triggering for survivors of domestic abuse and sexual assault. I hope this book can be a place where you feel seen and inspire you to reclaim your power.

Define Me

Scorpio Venus creator of love
metaphysical mystic maintains
worlds, spread grace
passion from pain.

The second puberty came
size 11 heels on a 5'4" frame
burgundy locs broad shoulders

carrying the love of transistors and elders,

Divine Protectors

Frances

Marsha

Sharon.

A collective blessing
squeeze,
itty bitty hormone titties
art on witchy fingers
a mustache paints my face.

To exist is not unique
no pain new
transform surviving into thriving.

I am a woman.

I define me.

A Father's Blessing

3

Bless me, Father
praise thy maker,

Play
a modern-day Abraham
caught in y2k.

End me, father
you're not unique.

A sacrilegious blessing
I inherit
Death's stressing.

Lemonade

Trapped in cellophane
he picks her;

Bright unblemished and ripe
he squeezes no bruises,
for the gift of burning lips

It's never enough...

Sour citrus flows
the drain drowns
lost again in cellophane

A hymn

5

Sing for me
show no glee
faith is
anxiety.

Pray now
die later
happiness awaits,
your Maker

Humpty Dumpty

It took time for the message, but she came. Years of shame were to blame.

My mother's heels came with pain. Holding my hands on my hips was strange. Gay was okay but Trans was deranged. Survival Mode, locked deep in my brain.

MJ, Angelica, and Dominique shined, and shame turned to gray. A cloudy reflection confused with reverence.

I traveled to "Nevada" and the dam cracked. An inside look at a Trans Experience, and I was certain.

A few years later, Eva came, and she showed me endless possibilities on and off screen. I was uplifted when I had no name.

Sharon Davis became my muse and shared her name. A legacy of love I wish to maintain.

Visibility and love the cure for shame. Trans is an identity I proudly claim.

My First Kiss

25:00,
14 hours after the church bells sang.

The lights of your SUV circle my house.

Mom outta town
dad drowned in sound.

"Still coming?"

My body shakes
in a frenzy,
I open the door
with scissors packed,
safety first.

A spot
hidden in the woods
where no one will see,
our kiss

whiskey, cigarettes, and mint,
rough beard scratches
my lips.

Unattained bliss lies
in a pool of piss.

Tragedy or Desire

Moonlight gazed upon your face
a 90s type of fine encased.

My heart pulled.

The morning tide reflected,
your wandering eyes (rejected)
closed
(Not)
braced

gentle fingers laced,
lips pushed, into
a simple embrace.

Conditional

9

Channel pain into verse
it's the way life flows.

Tolerant of intolerance
a lack
of good morals.

My breasts grow
and hands reach,
Incestuous touch
I know no peace

For the sake of y'all
I remain unseen

"Adults need to be…"

I fly, so I'll be free

Streetcar

The bully or the bullied
tragic life of man.

kicked down
court jester
The Clown

Tears beget violence
inner cries,
supposed silenced

corrupt conscience
needs guidance

Abuse is okay
"Blurred Lines" reign

Georgetown

We sat riverside
while the smoke passed between us
A star in the night sky
jet into focus.

Caught in wistful eyes
to carry among silent cries

a prayer, wish, and manifestation

a soft heart
and
a love so gentle
it surpasses dreams

Nostalgia Kills Don't Hate Yourself

A sea of regret
all lovers leave.

The wind whispers
sweet melodies,
once was will never be.

Embrace the tides
sail and sea,
she is me
so is he.

Forward,
back
a broken past
fluxed in cheap
stained glass.

Stay,
It's written in scripture
life's your destiny

Life with You

Quiet became violence
unread texts always giant

no me time was science
no space left to breathe

the sirens wailed
but I stayed,

your trauma consumed
my thoughts subdued

I finally learned too,
trust my intuition

discernment the key
Love is free.

Death

Last year we died together
I prophesied but was left surprised

21 was supposed to be the year,
but death came late,
draped in calico,
a shapeshifter.

Ink and ash stilettos marked our time to go
The last bed had no comforter

There were smiles that hid
throw-up piles
Coughs, choking, and pills for three.

Lovers cried and doctors tried
but
Night came, the angels sang

Ding Dong Your Dad is Dead

My first abuser is dead,
his life cut short by his own hands.

"He was your father."

"He loved you so much when you were a baby."

Apathy swirls in the air

Childhood spared me the pain of remembering,
but salt poured into festered wounds.

"Don't talk about him it'll scare your friends
away."
"Don't cry, the world is already burdened with
enough tears."

Sadness,
the man whose blood I share is dead

Gratitude,
I'm no longer plagued by the boogeyman

Apathy,
I choose to settle

beloved son, absent father, and stranger
the standard for all my love

Elle

Little tab
hear my plea,
a new dimension
is what I need.

Be my friend
keep me safe
let the tears
grace my face.

An idealized mind
lies,
not surprised.

You're just like
the rest
I never left.

Zoloft and lsd
don't make
The world taste sweet.

Venemous Rage

Adults always told me that I was mature for my age, and I believed. I witnessed a wayward child and intervened. I did not know this was an act of violence. My humanity was molted and shown no kindness. Left alone with rage's guidance.

The venom flowed inside. It begged to get out, but the people who deserved its effects were immune. The venom searched and found me.

Skin boiled, a divine sensation, while my mind toiled. I traced and begged for it to weep. Did I not hate it enough to bleed? I crossed over again and again. Satisfied, I could rest behind closed doors. My skin left scared, emblazoned in a fury.

Crying is Freedom

When I was a child, I would cry and cry
But then, he came along, and the well ran dry
A wet face was only okay if somebody died

I danced with the wind, my hands flew freely
The shots poured like rain, your words cut
deeply
I didn't know boys couldn't live freely

I looked for love in all the wrong places
An assault or two well that's nothing new
Love never came from fingers' rough traces

I played in lavender, and that little boy died
My eyes welled high, I wept for the sky
A Lily grown from that young boy's cries

Fall

Gliding through, crimson trees
trains flying cinnamon leaves
savory smoke crinkled, breeze

Barren death, walks west
painful buds form smiles
pink and blue skies for miles

A Reminder

Never gentle
we are not the same

Share identities
left unclaimed.

Never befriend a fox
With a colonizer's brain

Unrequited Love

Only a broken locker shelf separated our hands.
It started like it always did—with
competition—as we wanted to see who could
break the shelf completely. Twisting and tugging
morphed into a rhythmic dance as we took turns
twirling each other. We could not stop laughing,
and I began to notice how much I loved the
sound. I loved hearing your laugh, making you
laugh, but notably, sharing laughter. Drawn into
your sapphire eyes, I knew I was in love with
you. My feelings must have shown on my face
because your smile faded. My feelings had
surpassed yours, and I understood that you
would not reciprocate them. Wanting to see you
smile again, to make the moment last forever, I
resigned myself to silence. It worked, and I got
to see your chipped radiant smile.
I should have known then I was in love with
you, but I was 12 and did not grasp the concept
of loving someone. Sure, my family always
ended a call with "I love you," but what did that
mean? Your friends broadcasted how you
blacked out and ran into a wall chipping your
tooth. My stomach sank. What made you black
out? Was it some chronic condition? What

would happen to your smile, and would your family be able to afford to fix your tooth? I entered the band room and saw you sitting alone in your dad's office. My mood dropped even more, registering that we would not exchange our usual banter. I played like normal, but my mind remained focused on you. On the bus, I apprehensively messaged you for an update. I did not want to overstep, but I had to get a direct update and offer support if needed. You told me you were fine, and I saw you the next day like normal. Your friends found your chipped tooth humorous, but I withdrew, unaware of how to laugh at your pain. Ignorant to the depth of my emotions.

I looked at the clock to see we only had five more minutes before the bell rang. Five more minutes before our moment would end, and I would not see or talk to you for the Summer. You had new friends, and it had long been clear that we were school-only "friends." The bell rang, and you left to talk to an Upperclassman. It already felt like Summer, and I hated it.

Fall came, and you made it known it would be your last year taking band. Your passion was choir, and you started dating an Upperclassman. I was happy for you, so I continued to conceal my feelings. Meanwhile, my frustrations with being the last chair grew, so I planned to quit the band after the semester finished. I planned on attending a technical campus the following year, so the end for me was inevitable. I told you my news expecting some kind of reaction, but you were stoic. We were both moving in new directions.

For one last hurrah, we decided to do Solo & Ensemble together. I went as a soloist the previous year, making it to States and placing. Still, I missed performing together, so I was eager to be a duo and confident in our abilities. Our arrogance and depleted enthusiasm meant we did not practice unlike my first time as a soloist. Your dad was in the room for the performance, and it felt like old times when we first fell in love with the trombone. Suddenly, I wished we made time to practice. The judges loved us anyway and applauded how well we played together—we were "captivating." The praise could only stem from years of rivalry and our undeniable chemistry. I knew we could have played better, but I wanted more than anything to get a 1, which would get us to States.

"Please, one more chance to perform together so we can keep making music."

I was optimistic about the judges' feedback, but we got a 2, and I was devastated. It felt like a complete failure from the year prior, but I knew it was deserved. There would not be another chance, and I had to live with the disappointment of an imperfect ending.

We did not see each other much after that. Your devotion to choir increased, and I learned that the cross-country team was not a safe space for me as I stepped into my Black queerness. You began wrestling in high school, but I stopped because it made me uncomfortable—not knowing why at the time. We took similar classes, but our schedules rarely matched. Even when they did, I was too shy to approach you. You made everyone around you comfortable, and I had fallen out of your orbit.

Communications Camp our senior year was the last time we spoke. Without our phones, the group conversed during our free time. A pansexual underclassman struggled to explain the difference between sexual orientations—not that he had to. I tried to sleep, but I could not let him drown alone since he seemed aloof to his predicament. Your face was not visible in the dark cabin, but I immediately recognized your voice when you spoke. I upped my attempts to explain and used Li Shang from Mulan (1998) as an example of pansexuality. Still, you did not see the difference, and I analyzed ways to get you and everyone else in the cabin to understand. I internalized it without comprehending the lesson of willful ignorance. I

felt incompetent and alone. The conversation
moved on, but your ignorance weighed in my
mind.

I never professed my emotions or the space you
took up in my head. What if I decided to thrive
instead of settling for a state of survival? If I
had, would it have changed anything? Would
you have seen me even when I did not yet see
myself? Would I still dream about you years
later whenever you post updates about your life?
What if, what if, what if? Your politics appear
leftist, but what got through to you when my
words had no effect? Some white "progressive"
at your evangelical college? You seem happy
and surrounded by love, but that is not
surprising. Our paths might cross again in
another lifetime, but in this one, you will remain,
my first love, unrequited.

SAY THEIR NAMES

Say their names

Ashley Burton

A'nee Johnson

Ashia Davis

Banko Brown

Camdyn Rider

Chanel Perez Ortiz

Chashay Henderson

Chyna Long

DéVonnie J'Rae Johnson

Dominic Dupree, Dominic Palace

Jacob Williamson

Jasmine "Star" Mack

KC Johnson

Koko Da Doll

Lisa Love

London Price

Luis Ángel Díaz Castro

Maria Jose Rivera Rivera

Sherlyn Marjorie

Tasiyah Woodland

Thomas "Tom-Tom" Robertson

Tortugita

Unique Banks—Alexsandra Unique

YOKO

Zachee Imanitwitaho

And to all who go unreported

May you find peace
Your siblings won't stop until justice is served.

www.ingramcontent.com/pod-product-compliance
Lightning Source LLC
LaVergne TN
LVHW010839200726